Survivors
True Stories About Real Kids

Elizabeth Murray

Zoë Kashner

Laura D'Angelo

Nancy Fitzgerald

Denise Willi

Cate Baily

John DiConsiglio

SCHOLASTIC INC.
New York Toronto London Auckland Sydney
Mexico City New Delhi Hong Kong Buenos Aires

**Compiled by
Noelle Morris**

**Cover photo
© Peggy Fox/Stone/Getty Images**

Contents

Introduction

This book is about survivors. It's about young people who didn't give up when life got tough. It's about teens who faced difficult situations and came out stronger.

In this collection, you'll find the story of Elizabeth. Elizabeth was living on the streets. She was begging for money. Then one day, she decided to make something of herself. Today, she's a student at Harvard University.

You'll also find the story of Corey. Corey was living a lie. Then, he decided to stand up to his school. He decided to tell the truth. He became the first openly gay high school football captain in the United States.

Like Elizabeth and Corey, the other teens profiled here prove something important. They prove that no matter what life sends your way, you can make it.

Floods threatened Kaleatha's home. A land mine explosion took Ibadate's legs. An airplane crash sent Erin and Adam through a wall of fire.

Yet each of these teens made it.

In fact, they did more than make it. They became heroes.

Take Press. His truck was hit by a drunk driver. His girlfriend was killed. He was seriously injured. He could have given up. But he recovered. And not only that—Press now speaks out against drinking and driving.

Think of Press whenever life throws something tough in your path. And think of Elizabeth, Corey, Kaleatha, Erin, Adam, Ibadate, and the other teens featured in this book. Their true stories show what teens can do.

Elizabeth was a homeless teenager in New York City. Now she's a student at a well-known university near Boston, Massachusetts.

My Life on the Streets

by Elizabeth Murray

When Elizabeth Murray's mother was hospitalized with AIDS, Elizabeth had nowhere to go. She was forced to sleep on park benches and beg for money. Then, Elizabeth decided to change her situation.

My mother was buried the day after Christmas in 1996. There was no money for a real funeral. There was no priest. There were just the cemetery workers sitting a few feet away. They were talking about sports and women. And they were waiting to put dirt on top of her.

My sister, a friend, and I stood there for about 10 minutes. We looked at her coffin. It was just a pine box. I saw my mom's name on the top. It was spelled wrong.

So my friend took out a marker and fixed it. He also wrote, "Beloved Mother, 1954–1996." Then he drew an angel.

I was 16. This was the lowest point in my life. But I didn't cry. I was thinking too much. At that moment, something in me changed.

My mom's death woke me up. It forced me to think about the way I was living. I saw that I had a short window of time to get my life together. I needed to go back to school. I needed to make a success of myself.

And you know what? I did it. But it wasn't easy.

I grew up with my sister, mother, and father. We lived in a poor neighborhood filled with drugs and crime. My parents were drug **addicts.**

We never had any food in the house. Everything was dirty. The drugs were everywhere. I used to see my parents shooting up cocaine. They didn't try to hide it.

The welfare checks were spent before they arrived. By the end of the month, my mother would have run up a bar tab. She borrowed

money from everyone she knew. She also sold whatever she could get her hands on. Once, she sold my sister's winter coat.

I spent a lot of nights at a 24-hour supermarket. I packed groceries for tips. I brought food home. I also went to self-service gas stations and pumped gas for tips.

My parents separated when I was about 13. I was put into a city youth center. I got out when I promised to live with my mother and godfather. But by then, my mother had developed full-blown AIDS.

She was put in the hospital. I didn't feel comfortable living with my godfather anymore. So I took everything I could fit into my backpack. I took all the money I had on me, which wasn't much. And at age 15, I headed out on my own.

I slept at friends' houses for a while. I would clean houses to earn the right to be there. But I would hear whispered conversations about me. I always felt like I was in the way.

When I couldn't sleep at someone's house, I slept on park benches. If it was cold, I rode the subway all night or slept in a hallway.

Sometimes I'd go a week or two without showering. Sometimes I cleaned myself up in the bathroom of a doughnut shop.

I also begged for money on the street. That was one of the hardest things. Some kids stared at me. Others laughed. And some counted their money in front of me.

Then my mother died. I decided to go back to high school. I studied all the time. I finished high school in two years.

During my senior year, I got a part-time job. I saved enough to share an apartment. Then I won a college **scholarship.** I decided that I wanted to go to Harvard.

Harvard stood for opportunity. So much had been denied me in the past. I didn't want any doors closed in the future.

In June, I got a letter from Harvard. I had been accepted. I started screaming, "I'm going to Harvard! I'm going to Harvard!"

I'm not angry with my parents. They cared very much about me. And I loved them back. They were addicts before my sister and I were born. They probably never should have had

kids. But I'm grateful to them. They showed me which way *not* to go.

I also have some good memories. I remember my mother tucking me into bed at night. I remember her singing.

If I could tell her anything today, I'd say, "Don't worry about me. I'm going to be fine. I thank you for everything. And I love you."

How did Elizabeth's parents' addiction affect her childhood? How does she feel about her parents now?

© Cary Herz/Liaison/Getty Images

Press at the scene of a car crash near Albuquerque, New Mexico. The accident took the life of his girlfriend Cheryl.

I Was the Victim of a Drunk Driver

by Press Narvaiz, as told to Zoë Kashner

Press Narvaiz's truck was stopped at a red light. Suddenly, it was struck by a drunk driver. At 17, Press was seriously injured. His girlfriend, Cheryl, was killed.

The evening of April 19, 1996, began as a regular Saturday night.

I was a senior in high school. I was out on a date with my girlfriend. Cheryl and I had only been together a few months. She was a wonderful person. She could light up any room with her energy and humor.

That night was her last night alive.

We were heading home from the movies. We stopped at a red light. A cop pulled up next to my truck. Cheryl joked about how we'd "better be careful."

Suddenly, out of nowhere, a huge truck slammed into us at 60 miles an hour. It crushed the back bed of my truck. And it smashed into the cab where Cheryl and I sat. The force pushed us through the intersection.

The first thing I remember feeling was confusion. Then I saw Cheryl. She was slumped over on her knees. She wasn't moving. That's when I knew something was really wrong.

I started yelling, "Wake up, Cheryl! Wake up!" She didn't wake up. I tried to move my arms and legs. But I couldn't.

At the hospital, I was still unable to move. After about 45 minutes, I heard my mom's voice in the hallway. "That can't be true!" she yelled.

Then she came in to see me. Her face was so pale. "Where's Cheryl, Mom?" I asked. She told me that Cheryl was dead. I couldn't believe it. I started screaming and yelling.

The doctors calmed me. I had to deal with my own injuries. They said they needed to operate right away. If they didn't, I could have permanent **paralysis.**

Before the surgery, I talked to Cheryl's

Press's truck after the fatal automobile accident.

Cheryl Rodgers was only 16 when she was killed by a drunk driver.

Courtesy Press Narvaiz

mom. She had just seen her daughter's body. She was crying.

I tried to apologize. I felt so guilty that Cheryl had died while she was out with me. But Cheryl's mom said it wasn't my fault.

After the surgery, I could feel my body again. But all I felt was pain. You know how it feels when your leg falls asleep? And when it's "waking up" there's a burning sensation? Well, my whole body was like that for weeks.

Finally, I could start moving. But I couldn't walk. I couldn't feed myself. I couldn't even use the bathroom on my own.

I started **rehabilitation.** It was really tough. I had been a varsity baseball player since eighth grade. So I could throw a pretty good fastball. My first day of rehab, I tried to throw a tennis ball. I could barely toss it five feet.

It took three months of physical therapy before I could walk on my own. I seem normal now. But there are still a few things I can't do.

Almost a year after Cheryl died, the man who hit us was brought to trial. That awful night, he was so drunk that he couldn't see or think straight.

I think he was truly sorry. I watched him crying at the trial. He apologized to Cheryl's family and to me.

In a way, I feel sorry for him. He has to think about what he did for the rest of his life. He's serving a seven-year sentence.

Now I speak to convicted drunk drivers. Some of them do crossword puzzles while I talk. Others sleep in the back of the room. But some

tell me they're never going to drink and drive again.

I only try to give them the same message I want to give to you. Be responsible for your life and the lives you might affect with your actions.

Press says that he feels sorry for the drunk driver. Do you? Why or why not?

Frank used to be a skinhead. Now he works with a hockey program that brings black kids and white kids together.

I Was a Violent Skinhead

by Frank Meeink, as told to Laura D'Angelo

Frank Meeink was a vicious skinhead. He wasted years hating and hurting others. Here, he tells how he learned how wrong his life was.

When I was 13, I got into a huge fight with my stepfather. I couldn't control my anger at him anymore. My mom sent me to live with my dad.

I felt totally alone. My dad and his new wife were never around. It seemed like there was no place for me. It seemed like nobody cared.

That summer, I went to live with my aunt. I shared a room with my cousin. He was a skinhead. He had skinhead friends. They all shaved their heads and wore black boots.

The skinheads treated me like a little

brother. They made me feel protected. I thought they were cool. They said that whites are superior. They said that all blacks, Jews, gays, and foreigners are evil.

By August, my head was shaved. My boots were black. And I was preaching white **supremacy** to anyone who would listen.

In the fall, I moved back in with my mom. When my skinhead friends visited me, we got drunk. We went on "beat downs." We targeted blacks and gays. We hit them with bricks, baseball bats, chains, knives, and box cutters. It wasn't long before I was kicked out of school.

I started going all around the country, hanging out with skinheads. I had a **swastika** tattooed on my neck. I went to stay with some skinheads I knew in Illinois. There, I fell in love with a skinhead girl named Carin.

One Christmas Eve, three of us got drunk. We kidnapped a guy. We tortured him for 14 hours. We kicked in his teeth. We put his head through a wall. Then, we warned him to keep his mouth shut. We let him go. He went straight to the cops.

Two weeks later, I was arrested. I was 17. So I was tried and convicted as an adult. I was terrified of prison.

On top of that, Carin wrote me with some news. I was going to be a father. "Congratulations! You got what you always wanted," she wrote. I wanted a baby. I wanted someone who would always love me.

In prison, I met a black guy named Abel. He invited me to a prayer group. At one point, I was holding hands with another black guy, praying. I remember thinking, "This feels just like my dad's hand."

I signed up for the basketball, soccer, and football teams. When I'd score a touchdown, the black guys would say, "Good run, white boy." They would hug me. This went against everything I believed.

The only other guy my age was black. His name was Little G. He worked with me in the chow hall. I told Little G that I was afraid Carin was cheating on me. He said, "Man, don't worry. She's waiting for you."

I got out of prison seven months later. I was

glad to see my old friends. But they'd say things like, "Blacks are worthless." I'd think, "What do they know?" They never met Abel or Little G. They probably had never met any black person.

But I didn't say anything. It was hard to admit that the people I admired were wrong.

Carin had left the skinhead movement. She was devoting herself to our daughter. It upset her that I was still hanging out with my old friends. Our relationship fell apart.

I was having a hard time finding a job. My swastika tattoo got in the way. I was shocked when this Jewish guy, Keith, hired me. I guess he figured I was a messed-up kid. He wanted to give me a second chance.

Keith was the first Jewish person I had ever known. I grew to love him. It made me sick that he might think I secretly hated him. I got my tattoo removed.

Then came the Oklahoma City bombing in 1996. I saw the photograph of a fireman carrying out a dead little girl. I cried for days. I knew how I would feel if I lost my daughter.

For the first time, I thought about all the

people I had hurt. I felt terrible. I knew I could never make it up to my victims. But I wanted to try to make it right.

I stopped hanging out with my skinhead friends. I grew out my hair. I threw away my boots. I came up with an idea to use sports to bring together black and white kids. I started working with kids in a program called Harmony Through Hockey.

I'm 24 now. I speak at high schools and colleges. I tell kids in hate groups that they're headed for a life of pain. I tell them they can't beat their own misery by hurting others.

I know I can never make up for the lives I've damaged. My victims paid a price for my hatred. I put so much bad stuff into the world. Now it's time to do something positive.

What was the key to Frank's turnaround? What made him finally realize that the skinhead life was wrong?

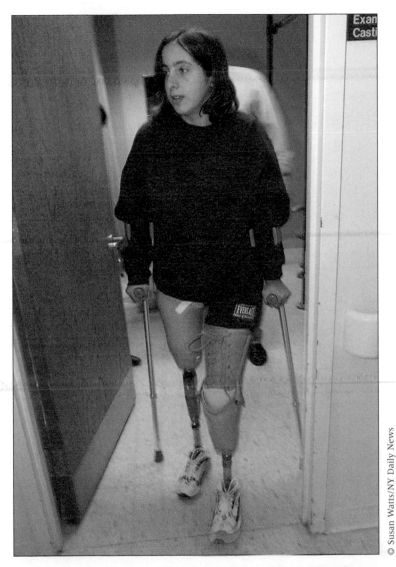

Ibadate Thaqi of Kosovo, Albania has learned to walk again
with the assistance of crutches and artificial limbs.

© Susan Watts/NY Daily News

Survivor of War:
Ibadate Thaqi

by Nancy Fitzgerald

Ibadate Thaqi lost her legs in a horrible war. But she kept her spirit.

She seems like any other 14-year-old girl. She listens to pop music. She likes to wear Old Navy sweatshirts and jeans. But Ibadate Thaqi has seen more violence than most people will ever see.

Ibadate is Albanian. She lived in a part of southern Europe called Kosovo. In January 1999, a war broke out there. The war was between the Serbs and the Albanians. "We were afraid that the Serbs would come and kill everyone," Ibadate remembers.

Everyone in her village ran from the Serbs. They set up camp in a nearby forest. "We lived in tents," Ibadate says. "When it rained, we

slept on wet blankets. Almost every day we had soup. We made it with things we found in the woods." Even worse, they could hear bombs dropping on their homes.

After three months, the Serbs left the area. Ibadate's family went home. They found their house had been burned down. Only two rooms were left.

Ibadate wanted to help clean up. She went outside to get a bucket. Under the bucket, there was a small bomb called a land mine. It blew up. Ibadate's life was changed forever.

"I saw myself with one leg blown off," says Ibadate. "And the other one was just holding on by a thread." Family and friends rushed her to the hospital. After surgery, Ibadate opened her eyes. She saw that she had lost both of her legs.

Ibadate could have given up. But she is a positive person. Soon she cheered up. Then she cheered up the other patients in the hospital.

"It was very hard," she says. "But I always thought that whatever happened, I can fix it. I'm a happy person. I would see other people with one leg or one arm were crying about their

A land mine. About 110 million land mines are hidden around the world. They can blow up 50 years after they are placed.

Ibadate and her mother at a hospital in New York City. There, Ibadate received artificial legs and learned to walk again.

lives. I would say to them, 'Why are you crying? We're alive!'"

An American reporter visited the hospital. He interviewed Ibadate for television. His report aired on ABC's *Nightline*. Then things began to happen. A **charity** group paid for Ibadate to come to New York City. She was brought to a hospital. There, she was given **artificial** legs.

For now, Ibadate is living with a family in New York. She is learning to use her new legs. "I remember when I first learned to walk again," she says. "It was a beautiful moment. Someone bought me a new pair of jeans. I looked like a normal kid again. I couldn't believe my eyes. I was so happy. I started crying."

These days, Ibadate has a lot to feel good about. Life in the United States is a wonder to her. She had never been to a shopping mall or a movie before.

"You can't compare life here to life in Kosovo," Ibadate says. "Back home we have no heat or hot water. We have no bathroom in our house. Life is much harder there. I think it will be hard to adjust when I go back."

Still, Ibadate is looking forward to going home. She wants to see her family and friends. She wants to return to school. When she gets home, she'll be a stronger person.

"When I saw what had happened to me, I thought I was handicapped for life." Ibadate says. "I saw myself as just somebody with no legs."

"But then I came here," she continues. "I saw the love and care of people who never knew me before. They were doing everything for me. I feel stronger. I have faith in God. And I have a lot of faith in me."

Ibadate has had many difficulties. But still, she has a positive attitude. How does she stay so positive?

Corey Johnson is captain of the football team in Topsfield, Massachusetts. He's with his mother, Ann Richardson.

Tackling the Truth:
Corey Johnson

by Denise Willi

Corey Johnson had a secret. For a long time, he was afraid that everyone would hate him if they found out the truth. Then, he decided to make a difference—and to make history.

Corey's troubles began in the sixth grade. That's when he realized he was different from his male friends. They were attracted to girls. He wasn't.

"In health class, a teacher told us that in every large group of friends, one turns out to be gay," Corey said. Corey wondered, "Why does that one person have to be me?" He wanted to live a "normal" life.

Then, when Corey was in high school, something happened that changed his life.

Corey's family was having a party. One of

his uncles pointed to a famous comedian and used a hateful gay **slur.** The uncle said gay people were "sick." Another uncle laughed.

Corey went to the bathroom and cried. Then, he got angry. And he decided to fight back. Slowly and carefully, Corey began to come out with the truth.

Soon, Corey shared his secret with three teachers he trusted. They accepted Corey for who he was.

Then, Corey found the strength to tell his parents. His stepfather, Rod, already knew. He had found one of Corey's emails to a gay friend, but never told anyone.

Corey's mom was surprised. But she responded to Corey in a loving way.

Corey's next step was to come out to the students in his school. Corey was worried how they would take it. He was really worried about how his football buddies would respond. He had just been voted co-captain.

Would his teammates still respect him as a player? Or would they think he was a sissy? Would they be afraid of Corey, especially in the

locker room? And how would other teams act?

If he came out, Corey would make history. He would become the first high school football captain in the United States to openly admit he was gay. He would break the **stereotype** of the macho football player. He would also break some stereotypes about gays.

"I wanted to prove that you don't have to do drama or be a drum major to be gay," Corey said.

Corey also wanted to give other gay athletes hope. So he decided to tell his football team.

Corey worked with his teachers to figure out what to do. Corey's mother came to the meetings. She was worried about her son's safety. But she supported Corey.

"If I didn't," his mother said, "I would be acting as if we were ashamed of who he was."

Coach Jim Pugh was the first person Corey told. His coach was understanding. "This is a great kid with a mind of his own," he said. Together, they decided to call a team meeting.

Finally, the moment arrived. Corey stood before 20 teammates. There was total silence. Corey thought he was going to throw up.

"I wanted to let all of you guys know something about me," Corey said. "I am coming out as an openly gay student here at school. I'd love your support."

"I hope this won't change anything," Corey quickly added. "I didn't come on to you yesterday. I'm not going to do it now." There was more silence.

Corey tried to break the silence with humor. "Besides, who says you guys are good enough, anyhow?"

At first his teammates held back. "People didn't talk to me," Corey says. But over time, most of his teammates and friends stood by him.

"More than teammates, we're your friends. We know you're the same person," one teammate told him.

Not everyone was so kind. There were gay slurs written on lockers. One parent said that Corey should be removed as captain. But Corey's coach refused.

The night before a game, the captain of the other team shouted gay slurs. His coach benched him.

Then, during the game, another player shouted gay slurs in Corey's face. "I couldn't stop laughing," Corey said. "Here, I had come out to my teachers, my parents, and my team. And this guy thought he could **intimidate** me?"

Corey is aware that some gay people have been beaten up and even killed coming out with the truth. His courage made national headlines. His teammates and the way they accepted him were a major part of the story as well.

Today, Corey works with high school and college students to teach **tolerance.**

Both Corey and his teammates have been called courageous. In what way did they all show courage?

Kaleatha stands on the plot of land in Tarboro, North Carolina, where her house stood—before Hurricane Floyd destroyed it.

© Charles Register/Liaison/Getty Images

I Survived a Hurricane

by Kaleatha Vines, as told to Zoë Kashner

In September 1999, Hurricane Floyd dumped 60 inches of water on North Carolina. About 48,000 people had to seek emergency shelter. Kaleatha Vines, 14, saw her home destroyed, her town in chaos, and her best friend disappear.

The TV news ran constant flood warnings. But nobody in my town thought it would really happen. Soon, we learned how wrong we were.

On September 15, at 3 A.M., a policeman knocked on our door. He told us that the water was coming. A dam two miles behind our house was near the bursting point. They had to release it. They told us to get out.

My parents and I got in the car. We drove for a few minutes. Then, we turned around. "It's

not really going to flood," my dad said.

I barely slept that night.

By morning, the water had come. I looked out the window. I saw people walking by my house up to their knees in water.

"Mom, Dad, we need to get out! The water's rising!" I screamed.

I packed some clothes in my book bag. My parents grabbed a few things. We couldn't find our dog. But we had to leave.

We drove through the water to a shelter. I looked back at our house and cried. I had to leave my posters of Eve, Jada Pinkett, and Vivica Fox. I left all my school supplies, my books, everything.

The shelter was crowded. But I could not find my best friend, Maquita Heath. Only one question was in my mind. Did she survive?

I heard that the army was bringing some survivors to the shelter in helicopters. I went over to the football field. That's where the choppers were landing. I hoped I'd find Maquita there.

The helicopters sounded like thunder.

In 1999, these homes in Tarboro were submerged by floodwaters from Hurricane Floyd. Many were destroyed.

When they landed, people started streaming out of them. Everyone was soaking wet. Many people were crying. But there was no sign of Maquita. She didn't show up at all that day.

I called her house. The phone wasn't working. I thought she was dead.

I cried so hard about Maquita. She was my best friend. But my parents and I had to move on. The next night we drove to my aunt's apartment in town. The flood didn't damage

her home. But the town looked awful.

Everything was out of place. Houses had been lifted off of their **foundations** by the water. Trees had furniture hanging from their branches. The smell was horrible. There were dead fish and dead animals all over.

Finally, my family and I were allowed to go back to our house. We wanted to rescue some of our things. When we opened the door, we had to move furniture just to get in. All of the furniture had floated to the front door.

I could see my shoes in the living room. I just grabbed them and left. I couldn't bear to see my bedroom. Everything I'd ever owned was in that room. The water had destroyed it all.

One week later, I learned what happened to Maquita.

I found her by chance. I spotted her at a store in town. We ran to each other and hugged. Neither of us had any idea the other was alive.

I had found my friend. But I was about to lose my home. Our house had to be torn down. There was no way to fix the damage from the flood.

When it was time, we went over to watch.

A tractor broke our home apart. We'd been in that house ever since I was born. My mom was crying really hard.

I have advice for anyone who lives where a hurricane or flood is about to hit. Please **evacuate!** It's better to spend a night at a shelter than to put yourself at risk.

I think that's why so many people died. They didn't believe it was going to happen. But sadly, they were very wrong.

Fifty-two people died in the flood. Others didn't have anywhere to go after the shelter closed. We were able to get a new home. I'm very grateful for that.

Kaleatha's family didn't evacuate immediately. How does she feel about this?

Ana didn't think it was possible to change her life. But her English teacher—and a book—gave her the courage to try.

I Escaped a Violent Gang

by Ana*, as told to Cate Baily

Ana grew up in a gang. She didn't know any other way of life—until one special teacher showed her she had other choices.

Gang members don't snitch on each other. That is the **motto** I was raised on. So when I was called to the witness stand that day, I was planning to lie.

Paco was on trial. He was my main man from the gang. I'd seen him shoot and kill a teenage boy.

John was on trial for the same crime. He was a member of an enemy gang. He was completely innocent. I was the only witness. What I said would determine which one went to jail.

The lawyer started asking me questions.

*This name, and all the names in this article, have been changed.

I looked at Paco. He was calm because he was sure I would lie. I looked at John. Then, I looked at John's mother. She was crying because it looked like her son was going to jail.

I started thinking about my mom and all the times she'd cried. John's mother's tears became my mother's tears.

Something happened inside me. It went against everything I'd been taught my whole life. I told the truth. I said, "Paco did it."

That was in 1994. That's when I got out of the gang. I couldn't go back after what I did to Paco. I was 15. But my story starts way before then.

I was raised in gangs. My father was in a gang. My brother was in a gang. My uncles and cousins were in gangs. I didn't know anything else. I thought drive-by shootings, drug deals, and beatings were normal.

I joined the gang when I was 11 years old. I got "jumped in." That means I was beaten up by the other gang members.

First, three girls surrounded me. They hit me hard over and over. Then, all the girls in

the gang made a circle around me. They hit me and kicked me more.

Then, the guys came. About 20 guys lined up on one side. About 20 girls lined up on the other side. They left a path down the middle. I had to walk down that path, as they punched and kicked me. I had to be standing by the time I got to the end.

When I started down the path, my arm was already broken. It hurt so much. As I walked, they punched me in the ribs. Every time I fell down, they'd kick me. I thought I was going to pass out.

Toward the end of the path, I fell. They stepped on my leg and broke it. Somehow, I pulled myself up. I limped to the end of the line.

That was my **initiation.** It was what I had to do to prove that I would do anything for them.

Some people say that people join gangs because they want to fit in. To me, it was more of a survival tool. In my neighborhood, you need a gang to be able to back yourself up.

Before I turned 12, I'd been arrested for stealing cars, breaking curfew, and having drugs. Each time I was let go.

But when I was 13, I was arrested for having a weapon. I got sent to boot camp for eight months.

Boot camp was the worst experience of my life. We had to get up at five A.M. and take cold showers. The rooms were always cold. The guards would scream at me. They'd say, "You may be something on the street. But you're nothing in here!"

For months, I had a bad attitude. I got into fights with other girls. I talked back to the guards. They wouldn't let me see my mom until my behavior got better. In the eight months I was there, she could only visit me four times.

When I got out, I knew I never wanted to go back there. I had to go to school regularly, or I'd get sent back.

I hated school. I planned to drop out as soon as I could. To me, my life was "kickin' it" with my friends.

My ninth-grade English teacher, Ms.

Gruwell, changed all that. She took an interest in me. If I missed class, she asked where I'd been. She told me I could be the first one in my family to finish high school.

I thought she was crazy. I wasn't used to people being so nice to me. When you're in a gang, you think that other people don't care about you.

I told Ms. Gruwell to stay out of my business. But she kept at it. Soon, her words started to sink in.

I began to see that there were other things out there besides gang life. I began to see that I could have a future. I started thinking about getting out of the gang.

In Ms. Gruwell's class, I had to read *Anne Frank: The Diary of a Young Girl.* It's the story of a teenage girl in hiding from the Nazis during World War II. Anne's words had a major impact on me.

In the book, I came across the line: "I feel like a bird in a cage, and I wish I had the wings to fly away." I couldn't believe it. That was exactly how I felt. I wanted to get out of the

gang. But they don't let people out. They kill people who want out.

That book really changed me. Before I read *Anne Frank,* I didn't like anybody I didn't know. I thought if you didn't look like me, you didn't understand me.

But here was Anne, who was so different from me. She was Jewish. She lived 50 years before me. But we felt the same way.

I remained a "bird in a cage" until the day of the trial in 1994.

When I was called to the stand, I said, "Paco did it." I said it for myself, to get out of my cage. I said it for my mother and for Ms. Gruwell. I said it to end the violence in my life.

Paco looked at me in shock. As they took him away to serve his 25-year sentence, he said, "Of all the people in the gang, you're the last person I thought would **betray** me."

I feel guilty to this day. I feel guilty that Paco is in a jail cell because of what I said. But I know that telling the truth was the right thing to do.

After that, I left the gang. I got death threats. But no one came after me. I think they didn't

kill me because I have family in the gang.

Today, I am a freshman at a college in California. I plan to major in English. Then, I hope to get my Ph.D. in education. I want to be the Secretary of Education. I'd like to change the way kids get labeled in school as "dropouts" or "slow learners."

If gang members could see that they have different choices, maybe they'd get out too. I'm not a miracle. Anybody can get out.

Why did Ana decide to get out of her "cage"?

Surviving an Airplane Crash

by Erin Ashcraft and Adam Salmans,
as told to John DiConsiglio

On June 1, 1999, American Airlines flight 1420 crashed as it landed in Little Rock, Arkansas. Erin Ashcraft and Adam Salmans survived the crash—and they proved to be true heroes.

Erin Ashcraft had a bad feeling. It was a little after ten P.M. on June 1, 1999. Erin, 14, was with her sister, Cara, 11. They were waiting at the airport to board their flight.

They were flying from their home near Dallas, Texas. They were headed to their grandparents' place in Little Rock, Arkansas.

"Something was telling me not to get on that plane," Erin says. "As we were boarding the plane, I wanted to turn back. I wanted to tell my dad I wasn't going."

But Adam Salmans couldn't get on the plane fast enough. "I just wanted to get home," Adam says.

Adam, 15, was traveling with his mother and his eight-year-old sister, Samantha.

The flight quickly became a nightmare. After takeoff, the jet flew through a thunderstorm. Rain, hail, and strong winds hit the plane.

When the plane landed in Little Rock, it skidded. It slid down the runway and crashed into a tower.

Then the plane fell into the banks of the Arkansas River. It split in half and burst into flames. Nine people were killed. Eighty-eight others were hurt.

Erin and Adam described their experiences.

Erin: During the flight, I was in seat 16F. My sister Cara was in 16E. I was by the window. Cara was in the middle.

I looked out the window. I could see the lightning. There was a lot of rain. It was coming down really hard.

But as the flight went on, I relaxed. I thought,

Erin Ashcraft *(left)* and her sister Cara a month after the accident. Both girls suffered leg burns as a result of the crash.

"They know what they're doing."

We landed nosefirst. There was a jolt. I looked over at Cara and said, "That's not supposed to happen." The plane was still going very fast.

The plane kept going. I was thinking, "We should have stopped by now." You could feel the plane sliding and sort of wiggling.

And then: *Bam!*

I looked down and saw fire. It came up from beneath my seat. I lifted my legs, but it felt like

the fire was all around me.

I didn't know it, but the plane had completely broken in half, right behind us. A fuel tank exploded. I turned around. All I saw was a wall of fire.

I got really scared. I was thinking, "I'm going to die. This is it."

The plane was slanted. It was leaning back toward the fire behind us. It was filling up with smoke. You could barely see anything.

Cara and I were the last ones out in the aisle. People were pushing us back toward the fire. I was screaming at them, "Don't back up!" They were telling me to shut up.

I pushed Cara in front of me. We climbed over seats. People were screaming, "It's going to blow up!"

I saw this crack on the right side of the plane. I saw some adults squeezing sideways through it. So I grabbed Cara. I pushed her through the crack. Then I squeezed through and jumped out.

We must have fallen about 15 feet. I realized I was hurt. My leg was burned from the fire. And

the hail and rain hitting it stung like needles.

I felt like we were the only ones out there—me and Cara. I couldn't see anything. I couldn't hear anything.

They took us to an emergency station. There were all these people with cuts and blood and burns. It was like a war scene. My leg was throbbing. It was covered with these big orange bubbles.

Today, there are a lot of things that bring it all back. When someone lights a match, it reminds me of the smell of burned hair. I have had nightmares about fire and explosions.

But the crash also changed my life for the better. I appreciate things more.

Adam: We were in row 18, seats D, E, and F. The flight was very bumpy. But I didn't think anything about it.

My mother said, "I wish they'd put this plane down." And once we touched down, I said, "Well, you got your wish."

I heard this huge explosion. I could see the plane cracking into pieces right in front of me,

Adam Salmans received an award for his heroism during the crash. His mother and sister are sitting in the background.

in row 17. The front of the plane was going one way. We were going another.

I guess I was knocked out for a moment. When I came back, there was all this fire. I didn't see anyone around us. It was almost silent. It was **eerie.**

The people beside us didn't make it. The people in the row in front of us were dead.

I pulled off my seatbelt and fell forward, right through a hole onto the wing.

I was halfway down the wing when I turned around. I had thought my mother and Samantha were right behind me. But they weren't. Then I heard Samantha screaming.

When I looked back, the plane was on fire. I was so scared. But I guess I was just going on **adrenaline.** I ran up the wing. I went back into the plane. It was filled with smoke and fire. I didn't see my mom. But Samantha was still in her seat.

I picked Samantha up. I ran all the way down to the end of the wing with her. I told her to stay there. Then I turned back to get my mom.

I got about halfway up the wing. Then, I heard my mom yelling for me. Someone else had helped her out.

I ran back down the wing and grabbed Samantha. Mom and I started running away from the plane. We were in the river, hip-deep in water.

Then my mom's feet got tangled in the weeds. She said she couldn't keep going. She

© Andy Scott/Dallas Morning News/Corbis Sygma

When American Airlines flight 1420 crashed, the plane split in half. Erin and her sister were in row 16. Adam and his mother were on the other side of the plane, in row 18.

told us to leave her. I handed Samantha to another passenger and helped my mother.

We were out there for a long time. Then we saw the fire engines and ambulances. We all started yelling: "Help! Over here!"

I was burned on my right thigh, on the bottom of my leg, on my arm, and on my head. My burns have healed, but they left scars.

I've gotten a lot of attention from people all over. They call me a hero, and I guess I see myself as a hero. But it's kind of hard to talk about.

I heard about Erin, and we started writing letters to each other. I think that will help. She's close to my age, and she has been through it too. Other people tend to say the wrong things. They aren't being rude. They just don't understand.

What is a hero? Do you think Erin and Adam are heroes? Why or why not?

Glossary

addict *(noun)* a person who cannot give up doing or using something, like a drug

adrenaline *(noun)* a chemical produced by your body when you are excited, frightened, or angry

artificial *(adjective)* man-made

betray *(verb)* to do something disloyal

charity *(noun)* an organization that raises money to help people in need

eerie *(adjective)* strange and frightening

evacuate *(verb)* to move away from an area because it is dangerous

foundation *(noun)* a solid structure on which a building is built

initiation *(noun)* a ceremony to bring someone into a club or group

intimidate *(verb)* to frighten

motto *(noun)* a short statement that is meant to guide behavior or tell what someone believes or stands for

paralysis *(noun)* a loss of the power to move or feel a part of the body

rehabilitation *(noun)* a process of learning to use your body again, usually after an injury or sickness

scholarship *(noun)* a prize of money to pay for school

slur *(noun)* an insult

stereotype *(noun)* an overly simple picture or opinion of a person, group, or thing

supremacy *(noun)* the state of being great or the best

swastika *(noun)* a symbol of the Nazi Party in Germany. It's now also used as a symbol of aggression and hatred.

tolerance *(noun)* the willingness to respect or accept the customs, beliefs, and opinions of others